The Nature Kid's Guide to
TURTLES

RENATA MARIE

LP Media Inc. Publishing
Text copyright © 2023 by LP Media Inc.
All rights reserved.

No part of this book may be reproduced or transmitted in any form or by any means, electronic or mechanical, including photocopying, recording, or by an information storage and retrieval system — except by a reviewer who may quote brief passages in a review to be printed in a magazine or newspaper — without permission in writing from the publisher.

For information address LP Media Inc. Publishing,
3178 253rd Ave. NW, Isanti, MN 55040
www.lpmedia.org

Publication Data

Turtles
The Nature Kid's Guide to Turtles — First edition.

Summary: "Learn all about Turtles, the Nature Kid Way"
— Provided by publisher.

ISBN: 978-1-954288-71-3

[1. Turtles – Non-Fiction] I. Title.

Title: The Nature Kid's Guide to Turtles

CONTENTS

Seas and Streams 4
Tiny Turtles 6
Swimming Reptiles 8
Finding Food 10
Salty Snacks 12
Sharp Teeth 14
Safe Shells 16
Speedy Swimmers 18
Muddy Winters 20
Traveling Turtles 22
Sandy Nests 24
Cracking Shells 26
Race to the Water 28
Floating Homes 30
Turtles in Trouble 32
No More Nests 34
Mistaken Identity 36
Out to Sea 38

SEAS AND STREAMS

A Green sea turtle sails through the water.

Some turtles live in the sea. They live close to shore. They live in the open ocean. Other turtles live in **fresh water**. They live in wetlands, ponds, and lakes. They live in streams and rivers.

DID YOU KNOW? There are about 360 types of turtles. They swim in waters all around the world. The only continent they do not live on is Antarctica.

TINY TURTLES

FUN FACT!

Kemp's Ridley turtles are the smallest sea turtles in the world. They are only two feet (0.6 m) long.

A tiny turtle crawls toward a muddy bog.

Turtles can be small.
Bog turtles are the smallest turtles in North America. They are only four inches (10 cm) long. They only weigh four ounces (113 g).

Bog turtle

Turtles can also be big. Leatherback turtles are the largest turtles in the world. They can be more than six feet (1.8 m) long and weigh more than 2000 pounds (907 kg).

Leatherback turtle

SWIMMING REPTILES

A Pig-Nosed turtle ducks under the water.

Turtles are reptiles. They have scaly skin. They breathe air. They are cold-blooded. They lay eggs.

Turtles have shells on their backs. They have beaks instead of teeth.

Sea turtles have **flippers**. Freshwater turtles have feet. Their toes are webbed. Both easily swim through the water.

DID YOU KNOW? Tortoises are a type of turtle, but they live on land. Their feet are not made for swimming.

FINDING FOOD

A Hawksbill turtle floats through the water. He is looking for food.

Turtles have sharp noses and eyes. They can see well under the water. But they can only see close things out of the water. Turtles can feel changes in the water with their ears. They can feel when danger and food are near.

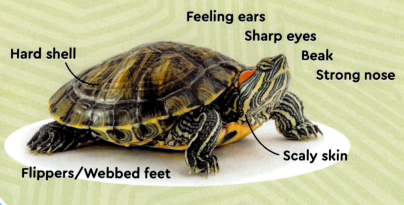

Feeling ears
Sharp eyes
Beak
Strong nose
Hard shell
Scaly skin
Flippers/Webbed feet

FUN FACT! Turtles can feel when their shells are touched.

SALTY SNACKS

Chomp! **A Hawksbill turtle snaps up a jellyfish.**

Some turtles eat plants. Others eat animals.

Freshwater turtles eat fish, snails, bugs, spiders, and worms. They eat birds, tadpoles, crayfish, and frogs. They eat fruit, algae, water lilies, and duckweed.

Sea turtles eat seagrasses, sea cucumbers, sea urchins, and seaweed. They eat crabs, shrimp, lobsters, fish, algae, conches, and horseshoe crabs. They even eat sponges and jellyfish.

FUN FACT! Loggerhead sea turtles have strong mouths that can break shells.

SHARP TEETH

Alligator · Bear · Bull Shark · Otter

Something big swims in the deep blue. It's a shark.

Predators hunt turtles. Adult sea turtles have to watch out for large sharks and killer whales.

Adult freshwater turtles have more predators. Birds and bears eat freshwater turtles. Raccoons, alligators, skunks, and otters eat them.

DID YOU KNOW? Snapping turtles can fight back. They quickly reach out their long necks. Their mouths are strong. Their bites are sharp.

SAFE SHELLS

Teeth close around a turtle, but the turtle's shell is strong. It keeps him safe.

Turtles have shells on their backs. Their shells are made of bone. They keep turtles safe from predators.

When freshwater turtles are attacked, they pull their heads into their shells. They pull their feet into their shells. They are safe.

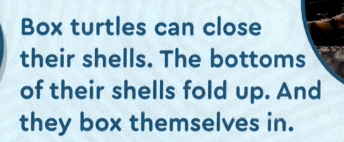

FUN FACT!

Box turtles can close their shells. The bottoms of their shells fold up. And they box themselves in.

SPEEDY SWIMMERS

A Leatherback sea turtle races to safety.

Sea turtles cannot pull their heads and flippers into their shells. **But they can swim fast.**

Leatherback sea turtles are the fastest turtles in the world. They can swim up to 22 miles (35 kilometers) per hour. They can dive 4,000 feet (1219 m) deep.

When sea turtles swim a lot, they need to breathe every few minutes. But when they rest, they only need to breathe every few hours.

FUN FACT! Leatherback sea turtles do not have hard shells. Their shells are rubbery.

MUDDY WINTERS

20

An Eastern Box turtle digs into the mud.

Turtles are **cold-blooded**. **As the water becomes cold, they become cold.** In winter, ponds and lakes are covered in ice. Turtles cannot survive in cold water.

Turtles swim down. They dig into the mud. The mud stays above freezing through the winter. There, their bodies slow down. They need less food. They get air from water flowing over their skin and mouths and even their bottoms.

FUN FACT!

In the summer, turtles sun themselves on logs. The sun makes their bodies warm.

21

TRAVELING TURTLES

A Flatback turtle crawls through the surf. She is on her way to lay eggs.

Sea turtles swim across the ocean. They swim to warmer waters. They swim to find food. Some can swim over 10,000 miles (16,093 km) each year. In the spring, they swim to nesting beaches. And they choose a turtle to make little turtles with.

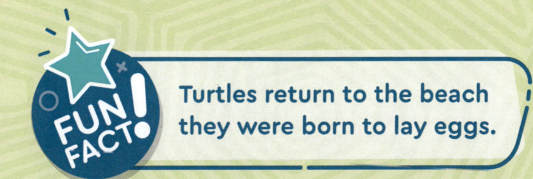

FUN FACT! Turtles return to the beach they were born to lay eggs.

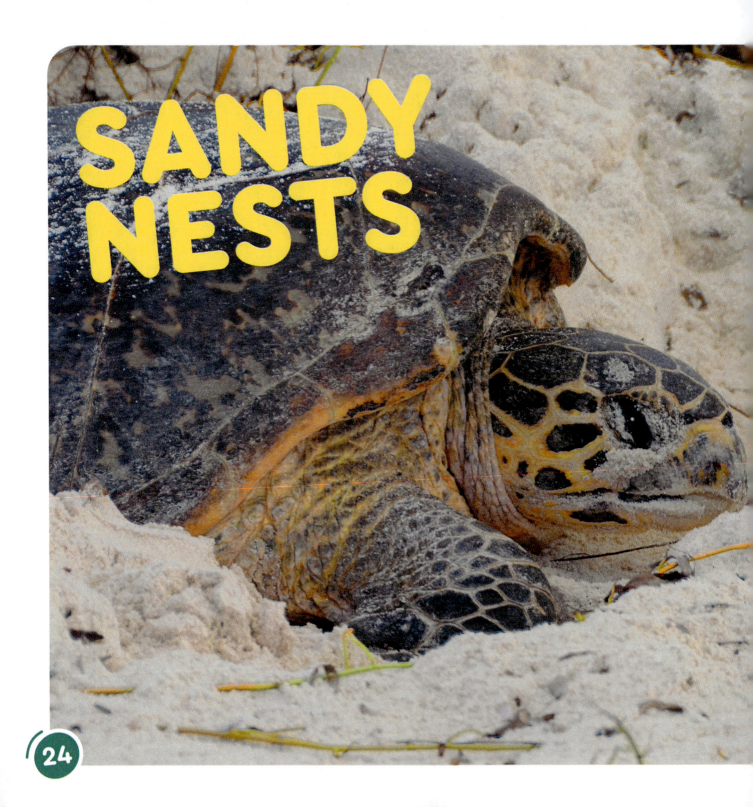

SANDY NESTS

Flippers toss sand. A Hawksbill turtle digs a nest.

Female turtles crawl onto land. They dig a nest with their flippers and feet. They lay eggs in the nest.

Some turtles only lay a few eggs. **Others can lay hundreds of eggs at once.** They can lay up to 10 groups of eggs in a nesting season. After laying the eggs, they cover the nests with sand and dirt and return to the water.

FUN FACT!

Hawksbill sea turtles can lay up to 200 eggs at once.

CRACKING SHELLS

26

A tiny turtle breaks through a shell.

Baby turtles are called hatchlings. Each hatchling has a tiny tooth on its beak. They crack their eggs open. Hatchlings are only about one inch (2.5 cm) long. They may take a few days to dig out of their nests.

Tiny turtles spill out of the nests. The light of the moon shines on the water. The hatchlings race for the light. They follow the beach down to the water. But they are not alone. The night is filled with hungry eyes.

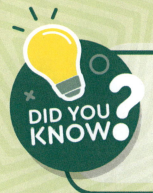

DID YOU KNOW? If the ground is hot, hatchlings will become females. If the ground is cold, they will become males.

RACE TO THE WATER

Hatchlings come out of their eggs. They instinctively know to race toward the ocean.

Many animals hunt turtle eggs and hatchlings. Birds, skunks, foxes, coyotes, raccoons, ants, fish, and crabs eat them.

Hatchling shells are soft. They cannot keep the baby turtles safe yet. The hatchlings crawl as fast as they can and slip into the water.

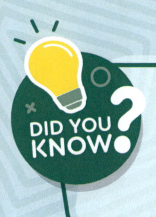

DID YOU KNOW? Earth is surrounded by a magnetic field and turtles can feel it. Turtles use it to know where they are in the open ocean.

FLOATING HOMES,

A tiny turtle floats on a seaweed mat.

Sea turtle hatchlings swim into deep water. Here, they are safer from predators.

The hatchlings crawl onto seaweed mats. The seaweed gives them a place to hide and find food. And they float across the ocean.

They will hopefully survive to be adults and return to have their own hatchlings.

DID YOU KNOW? Turtles can live to be over 100 years old.

TURTLES IN TROUBLE

A turtle ducks into his shell. But it cannot keep him safe from every danger.

Many turtles are in danger of dying out. The Earth is warming. Oceans are rising. Too many female turtles are being born. Garbage is blowing into the water. Humans hunt turtles. They sell wild turtles as pets. They build on their nesting lands.

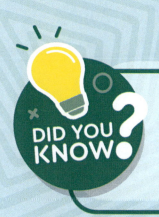

DID YOU KNOW?

There are only a few Yangtze Giant Softshell turtles left in the world.

NO MORE NESTS

DID YOU KNOW? Some people want special pets. They illegally **poach** freshwater turtles out of the wild.

A turtle swims back to her nesting place. But the beach is gone.

As the Earth warms, ice melts. Oceans rise. **Turtles are returning to nesting beaches that are underwater.** They cannot lay their eggs.

The sand warms. More turtles are born females. There are not enough males to make hatchlings with females.

People build on beaches. They take over nesting areas. Their buildings have bright lights. Hatchlings crawl away from the water.

MISTAKEN IDENTITY

A turtle bites a jellyfish. But it is not a jellyfish. It's a bag.

Garbage tossed on the ground blows into the water. **Turtles think plastic bags are jellyfish.** They try to eat them. They get hurt.

People spill oil into the water. The oil kills plants and animals that turtles eat. It can hurt turtles if they swallow it.

People fish with big nets. They catch turtles too.

People illegally hunt turtles. They want their eggs, skin, meat, and shells.

KIDS CAN HELP TURTLES

Do not use plastic straws

Do not use plastic bottles

Do not use plastic bags

OUT TO SEA

Lights turn off. A turtle safely crawls onto a beach.

People want to help turtles. They created a net that lets shrimp in and keeps turtles out. The turtles swim out of an opening in the net.

People made it illegal to harm turtles and their eggs. Some towns turn off lights at night. Then hatchlings go toward the water. They want turtles to sail safely into the open blue.

DID YOU KNOW? If a person sees a turtle on the beach, they should give it space. Turn off the lights. Do not take pictures with the flash on.

GLOSSARY

cold-blooded
an animal whose body temperature is the same as the air around it
page 21

instinctively
something an animal knows how to do at birth
page 29

flippers
parts of animals used to swim
page 9

poach
to illegally hunt or capture a wild animal
page 34

fresh water
bodies of water that are not salty
page 5

MORE AMAZING ANIMAL BOOKS from Nature Kids Publishing!

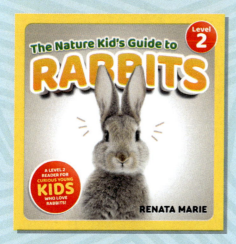

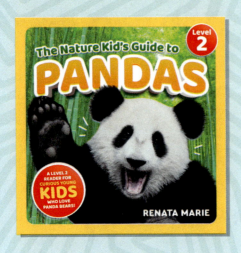

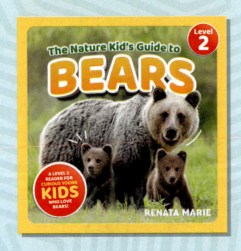

Visit NatureKidsPublishing.com to Learn More!

Made in the USA
Las Vegas, NV
10 January 2024